DISCOVER
Local and State Government

by Barbara Brannon

Table of Contents

Introduction 2

Chapter 1 What People Are in
Your Local Government? 4

Chapter 2 What People Are in
Your State Government? 10

Chapter 3 What Are the Three Branches
of State Government? 14

Conclusion 18

Concept Map 20

Glossary 22

Index 24

☆Introduction☆

Your **community** has a **government**. Your **state** has a government.

Executive Branch

branches

community

government

governor

mayor

state

See the Glossary on page 22.

3

What People Are in Your Local Government?

Your community has a local government.

▲ A community can be large.

▲ A community can be small.

Your local government has a **mayor.**

Mayor Shirley Franklin works in Atlanta.

Your local government has police officers.

▲ **This police officer works in Chicago.**

Your local government has firefighters.

▲ **These firefighters work in Springfield.**

Your local government has librarians.

▲ The librarians work at the library.

Your local government has park workers.

▲ The park workers work at the park.

Your local government has teachers.

▲ The teachers work in the schools.

What People Are in Your State Government?

Your state government has a **governor.**

▲ Governors help make state laws.

Your state government has representatives.

▲ **Representatives help make state laws.**

Your state government has judges.

▲ **Judges help solve problems about laws.**

What Are the Three Branches of State Government?

Your state government has three parts. Your state government has three **branches**.

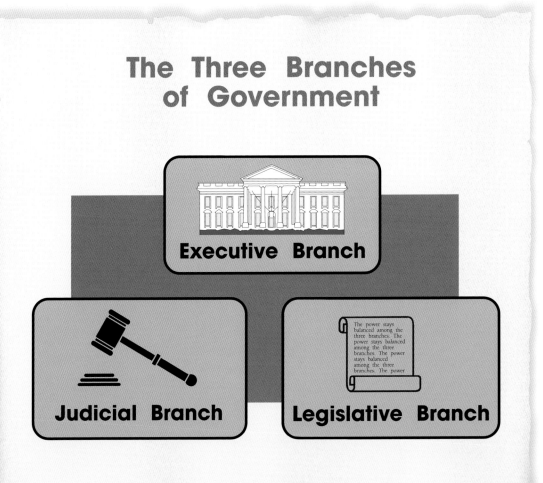

The Three Branches of Government

Executive Branch

Judicial Branch

Legislative Branch

The power stays balanced among the three branches. The power stays balanced among the three branches. The power stays balanced among the three branches. The power

Your state government has an executive branch.

Your state government has a legislative branch.

▲ Representatives are in the legislative branch.

Your state government has a judicial branch.

▲ **Judges are in the judicial branch.**

Your community has a local government.

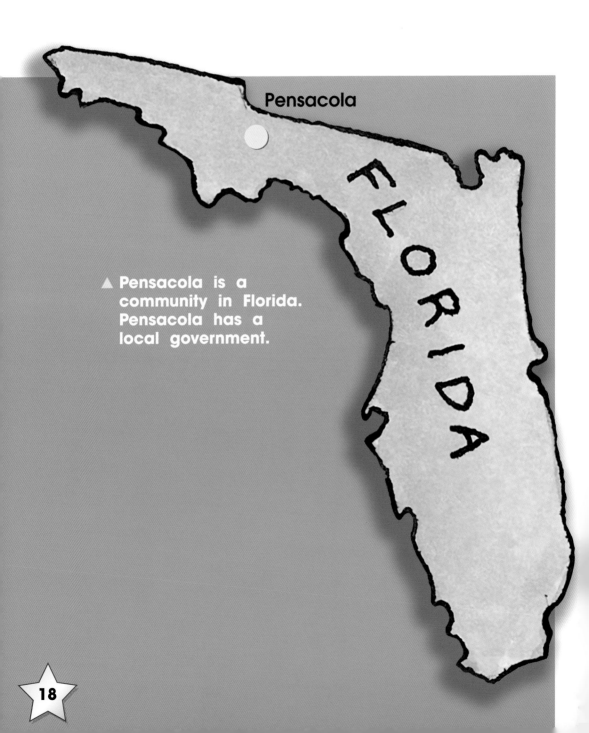

Pensacola

FLORIDA

▲ Pensacola is a community in Florida. Pensacola has a local government.

Your community has a state government.

▲ The state capital of Ohio is Columbus.
The state government is in the capital.

State

Executive Branch

governor

page 10

Local Government

mayor

page 6

police officers

page 7

firefighters

page 7

Government

Legislative Branch

representatives

page 12

Judicial Branch

judges

page 13

librarians

page 8

teachers

page 9

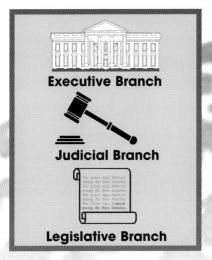

branches parts of government

*The state government has three **branches**.*

community a group of people

*Your **community** has a government.*

government the people who are in charge of laws

*State **government** has three parts.*

governor the leader of a state

*Your state has a **governor**.*

mayor the leader of a city or town

Your community has a ***mayor***.

state one of fifty parts of the United States

Your ***state*** *has a governor.*

branches, 14

community, 2, 4, 5, 18, 19

executive branch, 14, 15

firefighters, 7, 20

governor, 10, 15, 20

judges, 13, 17, 21

judicial branch, 14, 17

legislative branch, 14, 16

librarians, 8, 21

mayor, 6, 20

park workers, 8

police officers, 7, 20

representatives, 12, 16, 21

state, 2, 10, 12–17, 19, 21

teachers, 9, 21